# Guide for Class Leaders

# A Model for Christian Formation

Grace Bradford

**DISCIPLESHIP** RESOURCES

P.O. BOX 840 • NASHVILLE, TENNESSEE 37202-0840

www.discipleshipresources.org

Cover and book design by Sharon Anderson

ISBN 0-88177-274-7

Library of Congress Catalog Card No. 98-88821

DR274

# Contents

# Part 1

# The What and Why of Class Leaders

Jesus said to Simon Peter, "Simon son of John, do you love me more than these?" He said to him, "Yes, Lord; you know that I love you." Jesus said to him, "Feed my lambs."
**(John 21:15)**

## Introduction

If you are reading this book, perhaps you are already involved in church work. You attend services, serve on committees, sing in the choir, usher, or get involved in many other ways. You are busy doing the work of the church. Sometimes, however, we forget that our serving is for God through the church.

Why are we doing what we are doing? The work is often time-consuming and overwhelming, and we often find ourselves working alone. So why are we doing what we are doing? Probably because we realize that Jesus has assigned our mission as his followers—to make disciples. That's a *doing* mission, and much is involved in it. Jesus called us not only to do the work of God but also to be faithful children of God. Our method of serving God is not always balanced; we give much time and effort to doing and very little time preparing ourselves to *be*.

We know that there is much to be done right around us in our churches, homes, towns, and the world. And one person can make only a small difference, so we choose to focus on singing in the choir, greeting the parishioners on Sunday morning, or some other aspect of church work. We are hopeful that our contribution will make a difference in the life of someone who comes into the worship service. Someone, we pray, will hear God speaking to him or her. And our prayers are answered: someone does hear God speaking to him or her, even though we are not aware of it. "We see in a mirror, dimly" (1 Corinthians 13:12), but God has a view of all that takes place in our hearts.

I recommend the ministry of becoming a class leader as one that will give us a balance between doing and being and will help us use our commitment to help others find this balance. As we accept this ministry of discipleship, we acknowledge that God is working with us and through us to make all things new.

## Conversation With Self

I didn't give an immediate answer when I was asked by the pastor to become a class leader. I knew that as a member of a Covenant Discipleship Group, I was growing; and I also knew that, to paraphrase Luke 12:48b, from those whom God has given much, much is expected. For days I carried on a conversation with myself. This is how it went: "Why do I need to be a class leader? I've been doing church work all of my adult life. I've always directed a choir and worked with the Outreach Center, and I helped with the breakfast for homeless people for a period. I've coordinated Scripture reading; and on top of that, I'm in a Covenant Discipleship Group."

*That's why you are being called to be a class leader. As a Covenant Discipleship member, you are learning the discipline of being a disciple. You are learning the importance of watching over others in love, and you are beginning to serve God in a balanced way through your devotions, worship, compassion for others, and acts of justice. Now is the time for you to begin to help others do the same.*

"But I'm not that good yet. I hate to admit it, but my Scripture reading is sporadic, and there is still much I need to do in the area of justice. I'm not ready to take on that responsibility. Besides, someone may ask me, 'Who are you to help me on my spiritual journey?'"

*If not you, then who? Suppose every member feels the same? Someone has to step out on faith. Remember, you are not alone. Christ promised you that the Holy Spirit would be with you to guide you. You do call yourself a Christian, don't you?*

"Of course I do! I was baptized in this church many years ago."

*Then as a baptized Christian you are called by God to be a disciple and to make disciples. Jesus said to his disciples, "Go therefore and make disciples of all nations . . . And remember, I am with you always, to the end of the age" (Matthew 28:19-20).*

"Jesus' disciples were given that commission; I don't claim to be as good as they were."

*Jesus' disciples were laypeople, just like you, whom Jesus trained to be the leaders he would leave behind on earth to carry out his ministry. Throughout the ages God has called disciples to train other disciples so that the Word, like a seed, would take root and bloom in the lives of those who called themselves his children. This is your generation; now it is your turn. Will you do it?*

"Wow, this is a big assignment. I don't know where to start."

*If you want to be a disciple, then you can do it! Paul said, "I can do all things through him who strengthens me" (Philippians 4:13). Christ will strengthen you to be a leader among leaders.*

I finally had my answer. I knew what I had to do. "Yes," I said. "I'll be a class leader and try to follow the direction of Jesus."

## Jesus Gave the Direction

God sent his son, Jesus, to be our model. Jesus knew that people could not discipline themselves and stay on a righteous path with so many temptations around them, so he taught his followers and demonstrated to them how to be committed leaders of the people. He chose twelve ordinary men who agreed to follow him, leaving family and worldly goods behind.

I can do all things through him who strengthens me. (Philippians 4:13)

He taught them, giving them examples in parables; and when asked which of the commandments was the most important, he responded, "The first is, 'Hear, O Israel: the Lord our God, the Lord is one; you shall love the Lord your God with all your heart, and with all your soul, and with all your mind, and with all your strength.' The second is this, 'You shall love your neighbor as yourself'" (Mark 12:29-31b). When the lawyer asked who his neighbor was, Jesus told the story of the priest and the layperson who passed by the man who had been attacked and left to die on the street. It was a Samaritan who finally showed compassion and helped the man recover. He was the neighbor (Luke 10:29-37).

Jesus demonstrated how to love as he raised his friend Lazarus from the dead, fed the crowd of over five thousand with five loaves of bread and two fish, healed the leper, and offered living water to the woman at the well. Throughout his ministry he lifted up the disenfranchised, giving them hope and new life. Those who possessed demons were cleansed; blind and deaf people were made whole. Jesus was merciful and loving to those around him. He told the disciples and other followers about God's love for them and showed them how to put their trust in God.

Jesus also showed that he would serve others throughout his entire life and that his followers were to do the same. He said things like, "For the Son of Man came not to be served but to serve" (Mark 10:45), and "Whoever wants to be first must be last of all and servant of all" (Mark 9:35). He demonstrated this act of servitude at the Last Supper when he washed the disciples' feet. Though Peter protested, Jesus said, "Do you know what I have done to you? You call me Teacher and Lord—and you are right, for that is what I am. So if I, your Lord and Teacher, have washed your feet, you also ought to wash one another's feet. For I have set you an example, that you also should do as I have done to you. Very truly, I tell you, servants are not greater than their master, nor are messengers greater than the one who sent them" (John 13:12-16).

Following some of Jesus' demonstrations, he told the disciples that they could do all that he had done for others and more. He demonstrated to them how to pray and allowed God to be God through him as he accepted his crucifixion. Jesus was a disciple of his Father, developing disciples for his Father. He was a leader among the people, developing leaders for the people. His service to God and humankind came before anything else in his life.

Jesus also said, "Whoever comes to me and does not hate father and mother, wife and children, brothers and sisters, yes, and even life

"Do you know what I have done to you? You call me Teacher and Lord—and you are right, for that is what I am. So if I, your Lord and Teacher, have washed your feet, you also ought to wash one another's feet. For I have set you an example, that you also should do as I have done to you. Very truly, I tell you, servants are not greater than their master, nor are messengers greater than the one who sent them."
(John 13:12-16)

itself, cannot be my disciple. Whoever does not carry the cross and follow me cannot be my disciple" (Luke 14:26-27). In other words, "You cannot be my disciple unless you love me more than you love your father and mother, wife and children, brothers and sisters, and even your own life." Jesus carried his own cross and died to save us from our sins.

But Jesus was resurrected, and just before ascending into heaven Jesus met with the disciples for the last time and said, "All authority in heaven and on earth has been given to me. Go therefore and make disciples of all nations . . . teaching them to obey everything that I have commanded you. And remember, I am with you always, to the end of the age" (Matthew 28:18-20). Jesus taught the twelve disciples and the others who became his followers; he continues to teach us in so many ways.

## John Wesley's Model

John Wesley was recognized many centuries after Christ for creating a model for people who called themselves Christians. The model is based on the leadership that Christ demonstrated. A thorough account of these early beginnings of class leaders can be found in the book *Class Leaders: Recovering a Tradition* (Discipleship Resources, 1991). In it, author David Lowes Watson, a United Methodist minister, has adapted the traditional Methodist office of class leader for the church of today.

Wesley believed that people in the Church of England needed to be in small groups in order to develop a disciplined Christian lifestyle and at the same time watch over one another as they each tried to follow Jesus. He divided the membership into subgroups of twelve, called classes, with each class led by a class leader.

Wesley grouped the teachings of Christ into what he called the General Rules, a set of guidelines printed in pamphlet form for small groups to follow. The General Rules stipulated a balance between works of piety and works of mercy. The General Rules are still a part of the *Discipline* of The United Methodist Church. A copy of them can be found in section three of this book.

Class leaders were assigned to convene each class; direct the weekly meetings; inquire into the inward spiritual and physical state of each class member; and advise, reprove, comfort, or exhort each class member as the occasion required. They visited the sick, advised the pastor of any who were deemed as backsliding, and met the ministers and stewards in towns and cities and on the circuits as often as possible. In the meetings members gave account of their discipleship by sharing their experiences, praying together, and affirming or correcting one another. Contributions to the church were collected from delinquent members. Watson says, "The class meeting gave [members] a strong sense of identity as Christ's disciples in the world" (*Class Leaders: Recovering a Tradition*, by David Lowes Watson; © 1991 by Discipleship Resources, Nashville, TN; page 26).

Because of their methodical way of obeying the teachings of Jesus, these classes were given the nickname Methodist. Thus Wesley became recognized for founding the Methodist movement.

As churches grew stronger over the next two centuries, the role of class leaders was diminished, and the class meetings were discontinued. Sunday schools took over the teaching aspects, and other small groups provided the nurture that had been provided through the class meetings. Slowly the focus on accountability faded out of the picture, except in a few churches.

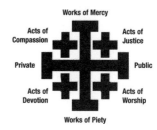

## Continuing the Tradition

The office of class leader has been kept alive in many African-American churches. Salem United Methodist Church in Harlem, New York City, organized classes and class leaders in 1902. This tradition has continued over the years. Although its organization is based on many of the rules of John Wesley, it is also based on the General Rule of Discipleship (see Rule in right column).

In a recent conversation with Gertrude Jackson, one of the class leaders at Salem United Methodist Church, I learned that each of twenty-nine class leaders is responsible for approximately twenty class members. The class leaders check on absent members, visit the sick, keep the pastor informed of pastoral needs, follow the General Rule of Discipleship, witness to members, and assist with members' problems. They maintain regular contact with members who live alone, taking them food, often getting them into hospitals, and helping them in any way that is needed.

Class leaders and class members were introduced in the Korean Church over a century ago. In 1986 there were thirty-five thousand organized class meetings in Korea, with three hundred thousand regular class members. Korean-American immigrant Methodist churches in the United States have brought the class system with them. Hae-Jong Kim, bishop of the Western New York and North Central conferences, has said in his book *Class Meetings Workbook for United Methodists* (self-printed; pages 13–20) that the classes have four implications for the life and work of Korean immigrant congregations: worship, fellowship, discipleship, and stewardship. Though the classes are led and taught mostly by laypeople and meet in members'

**The General Rule of Discipleship:**
To witness to Jesus Christ in the world, and to follow his teachings through acts of compassion, justice, worship, and devotion, under the guidance of the Holy Spirit.

homes, the class leaders are directly accountable to the pastor.

The tradition of class leaders and class meetings has been active in other parts of the world as well: South Africa, Zimbabwe, the United Kingdom, Australia, Norway, Germany, Austria, and Chile, to name a few. As the tradition dies out in some areas, it revitalizes and is introduced in others.

## Recovering the Tradition

In the early 1970's Dr. David Lowes Watson, looking back on the foundation on which The Methodist Church was built, recognized the need for structured discipleship growth for individuals. Drawing from the tradition of the class meetings, he introduced small accountability groups called Covenant Discipleship Groups. Covenant Discipleship Groups develop a group covenant based upon a contemporary restating of the General Rules as formulated by John Wesley. Known as the General Rule of Discipleship, the restating calls Christians "to witness to Jesus Christ in the world, and to follow his teachings through acts of compassion, justice, worship, and devotion, under the guidance of the Holy Spirit." Each group meets regularly, and the members hold one another accountable in Christian love to the covenant they have agreed upon. The Covenant Discipleship movement has given new structure to the office of class leader.

In 1988 the General Conference of The United Methodist Church restored classes, class leaders, and class meetings to the *Book of Discipline* after an absence of fifty years. The *Discipline* states, "A structure for **classes, class leaders**, and **class meetings** may be organized within the local congregation" (From *The Book of Discipline of The United Methodist Church—1996*. Copyright © 1996 by The United Methodist Publishing House. Used by permission. ¶261.). Since that time, Dr. Watson has been a lead advocate of how class leaders, under the supervision of the pastor, can nurture the spiritual discipline of small groups of church members.

In the new relationship between class leaders and class members, members are not required to attend classes. The leader communicates with each member (or family) individually. In addition to keeping abreast of the well-being of the class members, the class leader helps guide them on their spiritual journeys. This responsibility puts the class leader in a role of ministering to the members of the congregation.

## The Umbrella of Accountable Discipleship

Discipleship is an area of growth that is not only for adults. It should be introduced in childhood and nurtured throughout life so that one continues to be faithful and disciplined in following Christ. Discipleship is sometimes thought of as the same thing as being a Christian and is therefore sometimes overlooked and not always emphasized in Sunday school, confirmation classes, new membership classes, and baptism. Often Christians do not understand that God calls us to "go and make disciples" of ourselves and of others (Matthew 28:19, adapted).

For several years a committee of clergy and laypeople throughout the United States and other countries has met to look at the area of spiritual formation and accountability as it relates to all ages and to the development of whole people. This committee is called the Accountable Discipleship Council. The following groups have been formed using the General Rule of Discipleship and placed under the umbrella of Accountable Discipleship:

- Covenant Discipleship Groups—small groups of adults or youth that covenant together to help other group members be faithful in their discipleship;
- Class leaders—individuals selected to lead the spiritual growth of the entire congregation;
- Sprouts groups—Covenant Discipleship Groups for children grades 3 through 6.

The Accountable Discipleship Council, working with the General Board of Discipleship, is responsible for identifying and developing the resources to help people throughout Methodism and other denominations follow the path of Jesus. These resources include books, videos, newsletters, a website, training opportunities, and whatever other resources are necessary to help accomplish this mission.

## The Story of One Church

I am a member of Asbury United Methodist Church and have been involved in a variety of leadership roles. Asbury Church is located in downtown Washington, DC, near the White House, the convention center, government buildings, and many businesses. Most of our seventeen hundred members do not live in the church area but come from the far areas of the city, Northern Virginia, and areas south of Baltimore in Maryland.

In an effort to promote tithing among members, the church started an Every Member Visitation Campaign in which a committee was formed to visit members, discuss with members how the church could best serve them, and encourage greater giving. The financial emphasis of this campaign was less than successful, but much valuable information was gained, including the complaint that the church was more interested in the money than in the people. This raw, bristling accusation compelled the pastors and leaders to take another look at the mission of the church and the needs of the members. Were they related to each other?

The leaders admitted that although many members were active in service projects and ministry areas, many more attended only worship services and were not involved in serving others. Nor were they being nurtured by the church's ministries. We found that as leaders, we were lacking in our disciplined spiritual growth and in our ability to evaluate it. Moreover, the members of the congregation whom we were leading were not being intentionally guided in their own individual walks with God. The pastors couldn't do it all. We had to ask ourselves as a church, "Are we serious about following Jesus?" We were reminded to "strive first for the kingdom of God and his righteousness, and all [other] things will be given to you as well" (Matthew 6:33). Our concern for money was put aside, and the focus on our spiritual growth became the priority.

Our pastor, Dr. Eugene W. Matthews, invited Dr. David Lowes Watson to Asbury Church to discuss with interested members the importance of Covenant Discipleship Groups and class leaders. At the conclusion of that gathering of about fifty people, two Covenant Discipleship Groups were formed.

Four years later, seventeen groups had been formed to help members focus on their spiritual journeys. Individuals from these groups were invited by the pastor to become class leaders. They began the task of dividing the congregation into small groups of fifteen to twenty members who would be nurtured by the class leaders. The goal was set to have every church member in a class by the year 2000. Class leaders assisted their members in finding areas of devotion, worship, compassion, or justice on which to begin focusing. Monthly calls and visits by the class leaders provided information as to members' well-being, both physical and spiritual. Leaders encouraged, offered suggestions, and prayed for members of their classes.

Around the same time these programs started, DISCIPLE Bible studies and additional prayer groups were introduced. Since the inception of all of these nurturing ministries, noticeable changes have taken place in the church. The number of Covenant Discipleship Groups and class leaders has increased, there are few dropouts, and covenants among members of the groups have been revised to be more spiritually challenging. As Covenant Discipleship members and class leaders have accepted leadership positions over ministry areas, they have made prayer and devotions an emphasis in their meetings.

The ministries of these groups have begun to flow out of the devotional time together. Decisions are more spiritual, placing emphasis on consensual agreement rather than on majority rule; and there is more peaceful interaction on what could be problematic issues. The mission and ministry of the church is more defined.

Covenant Discipleship members and class leaders address the acts-of-compassion clauses in their covenants by working with some of the outreach ministries of the church. They can be found regularly distributing clothes at the Outreach Center, cooking and serving meals at breakfasts for homeless people, bagging nutritious meals for families in the food pantry, and passing out lunches on Saturdays and Sundays.

The goals of Covenant Discipleship and class leaders have not been fully met, but our church's mending is taking place; and the direction that these two groups have given us is helping us stay on course and follow Jesus Christ.

## Calling All Leaders

The need for leadership in the church is not new. We have known for centuries that in every group of people there are leaders and there are followers. There are also those who just have not taken the step forward to follow their calling. We can quickly recognize those in the congregation who have perceptive visions, who are passionate about their assignment, who put more time in on the task, who see new ways of approaching old problems, and who enjoy what they do. They are not always the ordained clergy; they are also among the laity, the people in the pews. Their actions are not about getting pay or recognition, but simply about recognizing the need and doing the best they can to serve God and their brothers and sisters in Christ.

Successful businesses have learned how to spot leaders within the work force and how to use them to help others gain knowledge and skill. Classroom teachers often use older and highly skilled students to help teach younger ones in specific areas. For the same reasons, churches need leaders to help new members, as well as older ones, learn what Christianity, baptism, ministry, and discipleship are about.

Membership classes are frequently organized to teach prospective new members United Methodist beliefs, the structure and organization of the church, and the order of service. The pastor and leaders in the church hope that these people will decide, "Yes! This is the church I want to join." Seasoned members greet them, have fellowship with them after services, and immediately try to put them to work.

*Those who are wise shall shine like the brightness of the sky, and those who lead many to righteousness, like the stars forever and ever.*
*(Daniel 12:3)*

Class leaders have heard Jesus saying to them, "Go and make disciples!" They may have asked themselves, "Who, me?" Yet they know that though they are struggling to stay on the path themselves, the Holy Spirit was sent to walk with them and with those they agree to help. And so they answer, "Yes, I will follow!"

"We need you in stewardship ministry!" "Come and join my United Methodist Men's group," or "We need you on the usher board." These introductory remarks are spoken quickly to new members before the next chairperson can reach them. Sometimes there is little consideration given for one's call, one's gifts and graces, one's interests, or the development of one's spiritual growth. In other words, discipleship acceptance and growth are left unnurtured.

Traditional work areas or ministry areas involve people in serving others, but they may not emphasize how to help one live as a Christian in a disciplined way. The new member must discover the path he must take and often journey alone, reading Scriptures occasionally and helping others when it easily fits into the schedule. As new members become slightly seasoned members, they are given leadership jobs over administrative and ministry areas. A three-hour to five-hour workshop in one day accompanied by the presentation of printed guidelines may be the extent of the training.

Discipleship is seldom the subject. Building disciples is perceived as the work of the pastor. Pastors, already overworked in the areas they were trained and ordained to do, cannot provide the individual presence that each member of the congregation needs for his or her spiritual growth. Pastors are also members of Covenant Discipleship Groups in order to grow in their own relationship with God. Both pastors and laypeople are called to walk with their brothers and sisters in witnessing for Christ. Class leaders can often be a present help in places and at times when pastors cannot.

## What's Your Answer?

In summary, class leaders are ordinary Christians who have decided to follow Jesus. They realize that they need discipline in doing so and want to be held accountable for their progress by others who will watch over them and journey with them. Class leaders have heard Jesus saying to them, "Go and make disciples!" They may have asked themselves, "Who, me?" Yet they know that though they are struggling to stay on the path themselves, the Holy Spirit was sent to walk with them and with those they agree to help. And so they answer, "Yes, I will follow!"

There may not be another source of concerned lay assistance for members of the congregation besides class leaders—no clear voice that will say regularly, "Missed you at church," "You are doing well in that area," "Here are some suggestions that may help you in your devotions," or "Let us pray for each other."

Class leaders will encounter some people who are not ready to be disciples, who are satisfied to come to church and be ministered to. Some will claim "more important" things they must do; some will say, "God is not calling me," or "Only the pastor can help me." But many pastors are recognizing their need for class leaders and are helping prepare them to lead in the congregation as co-ministers.

This manual is designed to help you become a class leader in your congregation. You will find the answers to these important questions:

- **What?** . . . as you read what Jesus directed followers to do;
- **Why?** . . . as you read the history of class leaders;
- **How?** . . . as you follow the step-by-step directions in this manual;
- **Where?** . . . as you look around you at the spiritual direction (or lack of it) in your congregation;
- **Who?** . . . as you go into your own quiet moments of spiritual introspection.

# Part 2

# Becoming a Class' Leader

And whatever you do,
in word or deed, do everything
in the name of the Lord.
(Colossians 3:17)

## Selection of Class Leaders

One of the first places a pastor may look for potential class leaders is in Covenant Discipleship Groups, if the church has organized these. These members have already claimed the desire to follow Christ and to be accountable for a lifetime spiritual journey. If such a group has not been organized, I would suggest that at least a pilot Covenant Discipleship Group be started so that a few members will gain understanding of and practice in how to grow continuously as disciples. Then they will model this for other members of the church.

David Closson reported in *Covenant Discipleship Quarterly* that at Asbury First United Methodist Church in Rochester, New York, a pilot Covenant Discipleship Group was started. That pilot group later began the process of organizing eight to ten new groups. Closson said, "We are learning that people are looking for opportunities to live more Christ-centered lives, that they yearn for a spiritual center to their lives, that they are looking for Christian structure and fellowship in their lives. The prospect of emerging class leaders for our membership and the 'ripple effect' of more covenant disciples in our church is exciting to envision" ("Invitation Accepted," in *Covenant Discipleship Quarterly*, Fall 1998; The General Board of Discipleship of The United Methodist Church; page 7).

In Covenant Discipleship Groups the journey starts with writing a covenant that includes clauses relating to acts of compassion, acts of devotion, acts of worship, and acts of justice. David Watson's book *Covenant Discipleship: Christian Formation Through Mutual Accountability* (Discipleship Resources, 1991) gives assistance in doing this. Once the covenant is written, the group meets each week for one hour to report on the faithfulness of each member in carrying out the covenant. After several months of attendance, the group members begin to see a change in themselves and in one another.

The pastor, who may visit groups from time to time, will begin to identify those who will make good class leaders. They are those who, in addition to being faithful to their own spiritual growth, will be able to help others on their journeys. Each person is at a different point in discipleship. Some have never considered themselves worthy of being called disciples and need the special attention a class leader can provide. Watson describes this relationship in *Class Leaders* by saying that class leaders have "oversight of a class of church members for the basics of their Christian living in the world." They are disciples, "complementing and undergirding the pastoral ministry of the clergy, thus freeing [the] pastor for the work he or she has been ordained and trained to do" (*Class Leaders: Recovering a Tradition*; page 98).

Dr. Eugene W. Matthews, pastor of Asbury United Methodist Church, describes the process of selecting class leaders:

This process includes a session with the class leader and Covenant Discipleship Coordinator during which we spend time perusing the names of people who are in the Covenant Discipleship Groups and trying to decide who should be invited to serve. Following our time together, and after prayerful reflection, I arrange for a time to meet with each person to ask them to consider joining the class leader team. If their response is yes, they are then invited to attend the next Class Leader Council meeting.

The responsibility of identifying people for congregational leadership is perhaps one of the most important aspects of pastoral ministry. This is especially true for selecting class leaders, because these people serve as an extension of the pastor's ministry. Therefore, the criteria for class leaders is related to their depth of faith, level of commitment, and openness to be held accountable for their discipleship.

There are also other places in the congregation whereby I have begun to seek class leaders. These locations are among people who are faithful in their attendance in Sunday school, DISCIPLE Bible classes, short-term Bible study, prayer groups, and other ministry groups of the church. In choosing class leaders from other areas of the congregation, we employ the same process used for class leaders from Covenant Discipleship Groups.

> The class leader makes a commitment, a covenant, to walk intentionally in the footsteps of Jesus, to help a group of parishioners do the same, and to watch over them with love.

It is not unusual for members of the congregation to recommend people for the pastor to consider as class leaders, for they may know these members personally or may have observed them closely in some area of ministry in the church or in the community. Phyllis Tyler says in *Guidelines for Leading Your Congregation: Leading as Class Leader 1997–2000* that the qualities of a class leader and any faithful Christian may be the same. The difference may simply be that the class leader makes a commitment, a covenant, to walk intentionally in the footsteps of Jesus, to help a group of parishioners do the same, and to watch over them with love. She adds that a class leader

1. desires to follow Christ in daily living
2. loves the gospel
3. is a member of a Covenant Discipleship Group
4. has the ability to empower others to be active Christian disciples
5. leads by example in Christian discipleship
6. is willing to be held accountable and to hold others accountable to the General Rule of Discipleship

7. is willing to contact fifteen to twenty class members by phone or in person on a monthly basis
8. has the ability to be a transformational leader, a visionary leader.

(*Guidelines for Leading Your Congregation: Leading as Class Leader 1997–2000*, by Phyllis Tyler. Copyright © 1996 by Abingdon Press. Used by permission. Page 16.)

## Taking the Next Step

The pastor has approached you and invited you to become a class leader. If you have been in a Covenant Discipleship Group, you have probably become disciplined in accounting for your growth. If you have come from another small group or were recommended by members of the congregation and have joined a Covenant Discipleship Group to round out your own discipline and accountability, you can be sure you have something to offer to others—the requirements of the office, your commitment to your Covenant Discipleship Group, your spiritual leadership in the church, and your love for God and for God's children.

If you receive a nudging from God to say yes, then do so. Obey your intuitive nudging. If you are not sure, take the time (a few days) to pray over it. The invitation does not require perfection of you; it only requires a sincere desire and commitment to continue to work on your own spiritual journey as you lovingly encourage others on theirs. In *A Plain Account of Christian Perfection*, John Wesley says, "One of the principal rules of religion is, to lose no occasion of serving God. And, since he is invisible to our eyes, we are to serve him in our neighbour; which he receives as if done to himself in person, standing visibly before us."

## Charge Conference Approval and Commissioning of Class Leaders

Each year the names of people who have been recommended by the pastor as class leaders are presented to the charge conference for approval.

This may be followed by the commissioning of class leaders within a worship service. The pastor invites the newly appointed class leaders to come forward and invites the congregation to affirm the class leaders' leadership and to accept their guidance. (See page 58 for a commissioning service.) The class leaders are now ready for service as class leaders and will begin by attending the meetings of the Council.

> One of the principal rules of religion is, to lose no occasion of serving God. And, since he is invisible to our eyes, we are to serve him in our neighbour; which he receives as if done to himself in person, standing visibly before us.
> —John Wesley

## Assembling a Class Leaders Council

The Class Leaders Council usually meets monthly. The purpose of the meeting is to report on the well-being of the council members and the people they serve and to provide spiritual direction for the work that is ahead. The pastor may assign the lay leader to coordinate council meetings. The pastor and lay leader will consult regularly on who the new class leaders will be and on any further business that needs to be communicated to the council.

## Agenda for Meetings

The Class Leaders Council meetings should allow gathering time for members to have fellowship with one another as they assemble. The group may decide to have light refreshments available before the meeting, but the preparation and service of meals should not diminish the real meaning and business of the meeting. The following order of meeting is based on the council meetings at Asbury United Methodist Church.

### 1. Opening

Prayer and devotions are offered by the leader or by an assigned member, and news of joys and sadness among the classes is shared.

### 2. Spiritual Direction

Spiritual direction is provided during this time by the pastor or by a person designated by the pastor. The purpose of this time is to help class leaders stay on course and stay motivated so that they, in turn, can give spiritual inspiration to their members, keeping them on course. This direction may come in the form of a prepared meditation based on Scripture, a Bible study, or a discussion of a current concern and its biblical implications.

As pastor and as a Covenant Discipleship member, Dr. Matthews of Asbury Church knows the struggles of other Covenant Discipleship members. He is aware of what class leaders need and is able to guide them spiritually in providing that help to members of their classes. The following statement on spiritual direction for class leaders is from Dr. Matthews.

> The Gospel of John, chapter twenty-one, presents a graphic scene of Jesus' resurrection appearance at the Sea of Tiberius. He gathered there with his disciples as an authentication of his resurrection and shared a breakfast meal. As they ate together, he startled Peter with the following inquiry, "Peter, do you love me?"

Peter blurted his reply immediately: "Yes, Lord, you know that I love you." Jesus then directed him to "feed my sheep."

Jesus was preparing Peter and the other disciples who had assembled to tend his followers, whom he called sheep, upon his absence from them. He was preparing them to love and care for the other believers. He was challenging them to make other disciples for Jesus Christ.

The office of class leader is similar to the shepherding model that Jesus commissioned Peter and others to demonstrate. Indeed a class leader is the extension of the pastoral ministry in the congregation. As Senior Pastor at Asbury United Methodist Church, I am deeply concerned for the spiritual care and feeding of the Asbury members and the constituents who are related to our congregation. Therefore, it is imperative that my presence be evident at every class leader team meeting on the first Saturday in the month at 8:30 A.M.

This portion of the meeting is led by myself or one of the other clergy of the staff, or a member of the congregation. This time is meant to be more than a devotional exercise; rather it should be a period to provide nourishment and spiritual underpinning to class leaders. This is necessary because of their responsibility to "feed the sheep."

John Wesley discovered that the office of class leader was an effective ministry relative for the extension of the pastoral nurture and oversight of the early societies and classes. Likewise, this ministry is just as relevant for accountable discipleship in our contemporary church.

At the heart of the spiritual direction moments is the biblical, theological-based guidance wherein the General Rule of Discipleship is reinforced: "To witness to Jesus Christ in the world, and to follow his teachings through acts of compassion, justice, worship, and devotion, under the guidance of the Holy Spirit."

### 3. Status of the Class Members

This report from the council members provides information on the spiritual and physical health of the class members and on any problems that need to be addressed. Discussion of class members need not involve the sharing of names or of information given to a class leader in privacy. Illness, death, loss of job, catastrophe, or other needs for prayer may be reported and may be followed up by the pastor.

"Simon son of John, do you love me?" He said to him, "Yes, Lord; you know that I love you." Jesus said to him, "Tend my sheep." (John 21:16)

### 4. Prayer for Class Members

This time of prayer should include those whose names or conditions have been lifted up. It is a time for giving thanks for the joys of members, for special blessings received, and for the well-being of the entire congregation. This is also a time to pray for strength to do God's will as class leaders and a time for quiet communion with God. The prayer may be offered by anyone in the class or by several people. Members should be encouraged to pray "unceasingly" for direction throughout the month ahead.

### 5. Assigning Church Members to Classes

Class assignments may be made at one of the first meetings, although changes in classes may need to be made from time to time. As new class leaders come into the council, they are given member assignments. It is important that each class leader also be assigned as a member of someone else's class so that his or her own spiritual nurturing may be addressed. As a result of poor health or other problems that may occur, a class leader may need assistance with his or her assignment or may need to be relieved of it temporarily or permanently.

Though not the only way to assign members to classes, perhaps the most feasible is by geographical areas. When class leaders are in the same area (community or zip code) as their members, they can visit them without too much traveling; or the class can come together occasionally if that is desired.

Ten to fifteen people and their families can easily be nurtured by one class leader. The ultimate goal is to have every church member, including pastors, in a class; but this may take time, for the process of identifying and training class leaders cannot be rushed. Setting a future year as a goal by which to accomplish this gives the church time to work toward this end.

### 6. Assigning People Who Are Not Church Members to Classes

There are people who attend services regularly but may not have immediate plans for joining the church. Family members, friends of members, people who help provide or receive outreach from the church, people temporarily living in the area who do not wish to change their church-home membership, and others also may need and want to be included in the classes.

Although the Outreach Center at Asbury United Methodist Church in Washington, DC, is run by members of the congregation, several non-member volunteers are just as loyal in their service to the center as are members. They may be assigned to a class.

Visitors who attend church on a regular basis and who have expressed interest in baptism also may be assigned to a class. Dan Benedict, Worship Resources Director for The General Board of Discipleship in Nashville, Tennessee, suggests that baptism should not be considered a private affair between the clergy and family. The entire congregation should take part in welcoming and helping to form the baptismal candidates as Christian disciples. This is an ongoing process beginning before and continuing after the rite of baptism. He describes this process as Christian initiation and says: "Christian initiation is the congregation's reaching out and receiving people, inviting, nurturing, and welcoming them into a pattern of appropriate spiritual formation. Initiation also entails opportunities to engage in ministry, learning, and fellowship that includes each person in the life and prayer of the church family." (*Come to the Waters: Baptism and Our Ministry of Welcoming Seekers and Making Disciples*. Copyright © 1996 Discipleship Resources. Used by permission. Pages 32–33.)

In reading the Baptismal Covenant, the congregation agrees to nurture new members in the Christian faith and life and to include them in our care. If the concept of preparing for baptism and continued spiritual formation after baptism is not familiar to the congregation, class leaders may take leadership in watching over new members with love and helping them understand their responsibilities as baptized members of God's family.

"What exactly does this mean?" the new members may ask. An appropriate response is, "We want to extend God's love to you by communicating with you regularly, rejoicing in your good news, praying with you over your concerns, and walking with you on your spiritual journey as one child of God walking with another. A class leader will be in regular contact with you."

### 7. New Business

New business may be brought to the group at this time. Sometimes a workshop or a visiting speaker who can shed light on one of the areas of the General Rule may be in order. A discussion of the class leader's responsibilities during John Wesley's time as compared to present responsibilities may put the direction in a clearer perspective. Upcoming related workshops provided by the district, conference, jurisdiction, or general church agencies will help members approach their own responsibility with new assurance. Class leaders cannot

"What exactly does this mean?" the new members may ask. An appropriate response is, "We want to extend God's love to you by communicating with you regularly, rejoicing in your good news, praying with you over your concerns, and walking with you on your spiritual journey as one child of God walking with another.

afford to allow their service to others to become stale, methodical, or dull. For just as God approaches our problems with newness, we must provide that newness for others.

### 8. *Sending Forth*

Final words of wisdom and a benediction may be given by the pastor or coordinator to send members forth into their world of ministry. Members should depart inspired and renewed in their love for God and in their love and service to their neighbors.

## Another Model

Dr. Mark W. Wethington, pastor of Southern Pines United Methodist Church in Southern Pines, North Carolina, shares the following information on the class leaders ministry at Duke Memorial United Methodist Church, where he served as pastor for six years.

There were five class leaders, who met monthly. Since there were not enough class leaders to service a congregation of nine hundred, we decided to concentrate on new members in order to use their time and energy effectively. Class leaders were selected by the pastor from Covenant Discipleship Groups and sent to a national class leaders training event.

I talked with new members about Covenant Discipleship, class leaders, and the General Rule of Discipleship and how we brought emphasis to that in the life of the church. New members were assigned a class leader who would visit with them and walk with them for a period of time to help integrate them into the life of the church and assist them in their discipleship in areas of piety and mercy. Some new members were already ingrained in the life of the church, were active in their community in areas of compassion and justice, and had a strong devotional and worship life. There was little the class leader had to do except follow up, making sure these members were finding a place of presence and ministry in the church.

Each class leader had four or five members at a time. The class leaders' responsibility to each person was for several months. At some point the members were asked if they wanted to remain with a class leader, go into a Covenant Discipleship Group, or at least continue to find ways to be accountable and grow in their discipleship.

Leaders were expected to give spiritual direction to class members, though they might not be any further along in their discipleship than the people they were trying to help. They too were struggling with issues of time, their devotional life, work, and issues of compassion. Their help was not about their own superiority in discipleship but about their "know-how." They knew where to go to feed the hungry and where to go to visit those in prisons, and they knew different ways of praying and fasting. They had lists of devotional resources and of compassion and justice resources in the community.

In regular monthly meetings organized by the leader of the class leaders, I spent time in prayer and devotions and presented new resources on how to form one's prayer life, devotional materials, and opportunities for service and compassion. Other class leaders were able to share things, too.

We kept the congregation aware of what was happening with Covenant Discipleship and class leaders in worship and in the newsletter. When someone joined the church, a class leader was called to stand with them. It was explained that this person would help guide them into the life and ministry of the church. The General Rule was printed weekly in the bulletin. We tried to make it clear that these were not pious snobs but simply people willing to find and develop techniques for being more faithful disciples.

## Getting to Know Class Members

The initial contact with members of the class is made through a letter from the class leader informing them of the purpose of the class leader ministry, the appointment by the pastor, and the responsibilities of leaders to class members. The letter may express the joy of the class leader to serve God and the congregation in this manner and the vision of the church's spiritual growth as a result of God's children helping one another. The letter should prepare the member for a call in the near future in which further explanation or opportunity for getting acquainted can take place. (See a sample letter on page 52.)

The follow-up, whether by visit or by telephone, allows the leader to reiterate the responsibility of the class leader to the member, including the help to be given in the area of spiritual direction.

The more direct contact the leaders have with their class members, the more they can learn about who they are, the security they have in their relationship to God, their understanding of Jesus' resurrection and its impact on their lives, and the unity they feel with the rest of the congregation and with the rest of the world. This information will help the leader assist each member in a special way. A leader may soon realize that among the class members, there are many gifts and graces. Romans 12:4-8 describes the gifts God bestows upon us:

> We are like the various parts of a human body. Each part gets its meaning from the body as a whole, not the other way around.

Our walk with Christ helps us develop the fruit of the Spirit: love, joy, peace, patience, kindness, generosity, faithfulness, gentleness, and self-control.

The body we're talking about is Christ's body of chosen people. Each of us finds our meaning and function as a part of his body. But as a chopped-off finger or cut-off toe we wouldn't amount to much, would we? So since we find ourselves fashioned into all these excellently formed and marvelously functioning parts in Christ's body, let's just go ahead and be what we were made to be, without enviously or pridefully comparing ourselves with each other, or trying to be something we aren't.

If you preach, just preach God's Message, nothing else; if you help, just help, don't take over; if you teach, stick to your teaching; if you give encouraging guidance, be careful that you don't get bossy; if you're put in charge, don't manipulate; if you're called to give aid to people in distress, keep your eyes open and be quick to respond; if you work with the disadvantaged, don't let yourself get irritated with them or depressed by them. Keep a smile on your face.

(*THE MESSAGE*)

However, in addition to our gifts we should also be aware that our walk with Christ helps us develop what Paul described in Galatians 5:22-23 as fruit of the Spirit: "love, joy, peace, patience, kindness, generosity, faithfulness, gentleness, and self-control." Eugene H. Peterson describes it in another way:

But what happens when we live God's way? He brings gifts into our lives, much the same way that fruit appears in an orchard—things like affection for others, exuberance about life, serenity. We develop a willingness to stick with things, a sense of compassion in the heart, and a conviction that a basic holiness permeates things and people. We find ourselves involved in loyal commitments, not needing to force our way in life, able to marshal and direct our energies wisely.

(*THE MESSAGE*)

David Watson points out in *Class Leaders* that people who have gifts may not have the graces; likewise, those with graces may not have the gifts. He says, "Obedience to Jesus Christ, following his teachings step by step and day by day, does not depend on the extent of our spiritual gifts, but rather on doing the best we can with the gifts we have been given" (*Class Leaders: Recovering a Tradition*; pages 109–110). While our gifts that depend on our doing lead us to accepting easily the acts of compassion and acts of justice in the General Rule of Discipleship, the fruits of the Spirit grow into our being as a result of our faithfulness to God.

Often people are not aware of their gifts or graces. It may be easy to discern them in others but not in oneself. Through regular conversations, class leaders may recognize and point out to members their strong points, helping them decide for themselves where they can best serve the congregation and community.

Sometimes entire families are assigned to class leaders. It is not always necessary for class leaders to talk with each member of the family on a regular basis. One person may be the regular contact by phone; but talking briefly with other family members, particularly children, at various times conveys to them the leader's interest in each person and the recognition that each is a part of the body.

It is not unusual for members to share their joys with the class leader. News of graduations, new jobs, birthday celebrations, anniversaries, and other special events allows the leader to rejoice in the goodness of God along with the family members. Sending cards, talking to the person involved, and being present at special events allow the leader to walk closer with the family.

Class leaders are not expected to provide advice or solutions but to remind members of the presence of God in all situations. Inspirational encouragement—in the form of a relevant passage of Scripture, a poem, a hymn, or a personal story of how the Holy Spirit stepped in when all else seemed hopeless—can cheer a person up. Sometimes all a person needs is for someone to listen. This personal attention may provide the hope that is needed to get through the day and into the next one; another day may bring another perspective. Some concerns, questions, or complaints need to be addressed specifically by the pastor or lay leader. The class leader passes these concerns on to the pastor either in the class leaders meeting or privately.

## Keeping in Touch

Although it is ideal for class leaders to have face-to-face visits with members, that is not always possible. Any visits that do occur should be preceded by a phone call.

For various reasons, class members may not wish to have their leader visit, and it is important to respect their wishes. Weekly or monthly phone calls can be just as effective as visits. The agenda for a phone call would include the type of conversation one would have with a friend—inquiry into the health of family members, exchange of joys, or whatever else the member wishes to share. There may be an expression of concern if the member has not been seen at church; however, a listening ear is preferred over a prying attitude. As the leader gets to know each member, the contact with each will become more personal and individualized.

A discussion concerning the spiritual journeys of both the leader and member may take place, followed by a prayer for the success of both.

The rapid increase in communication technology provides new ways of keeping in touch with members. If leader and member have e-mail capabilities, they may choose this mode for occasional or frequent communication. E-mail allows for informal talk, quick conversation, reminders, frequent checking in, and opportunity to still be in touch when either is out of town. Some e-mail carriers offer buddy lists that make it possible for a group of friends to chat regularly at will.

## Helping Members With Their Spiritual Direction

After several conversations that allow leader and member to become better acquainted and more comfortable talking with each other, the discussion of spiritual direction will not be awkward. The leader explains again that as a class leader trying to be faithful in his or her journey with Christ, he or she will help the members of the group do the same. The class leader discusses the leader's membership in a Covenant Discipleship class, the writing of the covenant, and the accountability of the members as they strive to be disciples of Christ. The class leader points out the General Rule of Discipleship, providing a copy to the member:

> **To witness to Jesus Christ in the world, and to follow his teachings through acts of compassion, justice, worship, and devotion, under the guidance of the Holy Spirit.**

### 1. Acts of Devotion

This is often a good starting point for class members, for we often neglect it in our busy lives or practice a form of devotions-on-the-run. We need to spend more time with God than the usual two hours in church on Sunday. Reporting to God on a regular, daily, intentional basis helps us in being led regularly by the Holy Spirit. Devotions include our time for prayer, Scripture reading, other inspirational readings, meditation, and especially time for listening to God.

When we pray in the morning, we recognize the need to prepare ourselves for all that the day will bring. When we pray in the evening, it is for thanksgiving for blessings received during the day and for the understanding that all happenings are blessings. Praying throughout the day keeps our minds focused on God and on others. Reading and studying Scripture, with particular emphasis on the New Testament (whether it is one verse or one chapter), gives us a clearer understanding of the work we are to do as disciples.

In the course of the day there will be moments of tension, fear, joy, peace, relationship problems, disappointment, recognized grace, and spiritual revelations. At times we may be tempted to respond angrily to someone, particularly if that person is acting negatively toward us. By arming ourselves with a period of devotion, we are calmer at the moment of trial and able to respond lovingly.

## 2. Acts of Worship

Acts of worship should focus on improving our church attendance, appreciating the opportunity to tithe to God, and participating in regular Holy Communion. They should also help us to be more mindful of the role we play individually in the baptism of others, to remember our own baptism, and to understand and acknowledge the special meanings of the seasons of the church year. The corporate worship time we spend with others binds us in unity with them. Where two or three are gathered in Jesus' name, there is power and strength because the Holy Spirit is there also (Matthew 18:20, paraphrased). We begin to evaluate our worship participation, asking ourselves, *Do I attend worship services regularly? Do I make the worship service meaningful to me? Am I using my talents in the ministry of worship?* Worship becomes vital, for we realize that it is a time for refueling.

## 3. Acts of Compassion

These acts involve us in seeing all people as children of God. Therefore, we can look our sisters and brothers in Christ in the eyes as we see them homeless on the streets, partaking of gifts from our church food pantries, and sitting beside us in worship. We can involve ourselves in prison or shelter ministries, programs to help children and teenagers, and visitation at nursing homes and other institutions needing volunteer assistance. We can become more patient, understanding, and forgiving of the people around us.

## 4. Acts of Justice

Acts of justice evolve out of "why" questions; for example, What is the root of homelessness? Why do we need soup kitchens? Why are there so many abused children? How can I address the cause?
As practicing disciples we are alert to issues of justice for all people in the home, the workplace, the church, and the world. We readily speak out against discrimination of all types: race, religion, gender, and abilities.

Phyllis Tyler says:

> These four areas of justice, compassion, devotion, and worship interact with each other and complement each other. For

example, acts of justice will be grounded in a firmer foundation if prayer is used at each step toward a recovery of justice. These acts may begin with simple steps of compassion, such as addressing the root causes of hunger by asking, "Why do certain racial groups have less money?" Likewise, reading the Scriptures will be better understood if the one reading is engaged in works of justice and compassion, and vice versa. If held in tension with each other, the works of devotion and worship relate to compassion and justice and will help persons to grow as whole and active Christian disciples.

(Guidelines for Leading Your Congregation:<br>Leading as Class Leader 1997–2000; page 12.)

Even though the majority of people in the congregation may not be in Covenant Discipleship Groups, the class leader realizes that the General Rule of Discipleship is a starting point for class members who want to improve in their discipleship. Addressing one clause at a time is sufficient. In this and future discussions, the acts of devotion, worship, compassion, and justice can be discussed. Members should be encouraged to join a Covenant Discipleship Group or to decide one area of the General Rule, and specifically one clause, that they would like to begin to work on. A sample of a conversation that may take place is as follows:

"Is there an area of your devotions that is not as strong or as committed as you would like?" the class leader asks.

"No, I can't think of anything right now," the member may answer.

"Are you satisfied that you are reading the Bible regularly or praying regularly for others?"

"I read the Bible occasionally, but I can't say that I do on a regular basis. I just can't seem to find the time."

"Would you like to work on this area of your devotions? You can start with short passages. Reading a short passage that you can contemplate during the day is a way of getting started."

"Yes, I could do that. But I wouldn't know where to start."

"I can send you some Lectionary resources for daily reading, or you can just start with a devotional book such as *The Upper Room*. I've started reading about the life of Jesus according to the Book of Luke. Though my covenant clause says I will read Scripture daily, I must admit I'm not as regular as I would like to be. This is something we can help each other with. I will remind and encourage you, and I would appreciate you encouraging me so that we will both remain faithful to our study of the Word."

In this conversation, the leader points out that he is not an authority but simply one striving to follow Christ and to learn more about the Christian way. He also conveys that he and the class member can help each other through encouragement and even providing resources. Adding a time commitment such as "daily" or "regularly" helps one to stay on track. The leader should not overwhelm the member by introducing several clauses initially. One at a time is sufficient until the member is ready to include another or to join a Covenant Discipleship Group. The leader may help the member put the commitment into a clause such as, "I will read the Bible at least three times a week." If the spiritual direction sounds easy enough to follow, the member will eagerly agree, "I can do that."

Subsequent calls may allow the leader to inquire, "How are you doing on your Bible reading?" Suggestions may be made if needed as to time of day, length of passage, or even using a journal to follow up thoughts on the passage.

When the member is proceeding satisfactorily with this area of focus, the leader may want to suggest that the member consider adding another area of focus. "Are you getting to worship service on a regular basis? Is this an area in which you would like to improve?"

The leader may want to send the member a sample list of clauses (see page 50), loan a book, or suggest other resources. Members may find it easier to start with an area in which they feel somewhat comfortable. If they are already working in the area of compassion by participating regularly with dinners for people who are homeless, they may balance this out by praying for the people they serve in their time of devotions or even praying for the people inwardly as they are serving them. They may address the justice issue by speaking out for better conditions for homeless people.

## Receiving Guidance From the Holy Spirit

Class leaders are not expected to have all the answers. I know I don't. But the good news is that we are not alone. This important work is the work of God. Just as Moses realized he had to return to God regularly for direction in leading the Israelites out of Egypt and to the Promised Land, we too must go into the silence on a regular basis to receive guidance on all aspects of our lives, particularly those areas we recognize as our ministry. One of the values of being in Covenant Discipleship Groups is that we learn that we must be faithful to our own periods of devotions. As class leaders, our devotional period must be intentional. It should include

- reading the Bible regularly and meditating on it, letting it speak to our daily activities;

- praying by thanking God for each day's opportunities and for the ministries that our gifts and graces provide us; praying for the people in our classes and other people we know or do not know during the day; and asking forgiveness for ourselves and for others. Paul urged us to pray without ceasing, to stay open for conversation with God all during the day.
- reading other inspirational and devotional materials;
- spending time daily in silence. Talking to God is not the same as listening to God. Even when there appears to be no conversation, God is there.

There is always a question of time. But time, like a tithe, should be taken off the top. It should be planned and scheduled into the day just as eating and watching television are.

## A Connecting Point

We must share with our members our own need to seek God regularly and our own desire to walk in the ways of Jesus, to love all creatures great and small, to feed "the sheep," to clothe the naked, to visit those imprisoned, and to speak up for justice. This is why we are Christians; this is why we joined Covenant Discipleship Groups; this is why we are class leaders—so that we will walk the path a little straighter each day. And we realize we cannot walk alone. The relationship between class leader and class member is one of walking together, encouraging each other.

## Meeting Objections

Some members will welcome your interest in them and will want to be encouraged in their spiritual growth. However, all members cannot be expected to quickly grasp the idea of the class leader/class member relationship. Some may be suspicious of the motive of class leaders. Some may resent sharing their private spiritual life. It may not be easy for a person to admit, "I seldom read the Bible," or "I don't have time for devotions." A pastor recently related some objections he has received from his congregation: "No one wanted to be seen as spiritually superior to another. Some were concerned with the word *class*. Some were uncomfortable with class meetings."

Other responses that may be heard from members include
- "I'm doing fine; I don't need help."
- "Yes, I read the Bible and pray as often as I can."
- "I don't see how one person can help another; none of us is perfect."

- "My walk with God is a personal one."
- "I attend church regularly and give my services. That's enough for me."
- "Who are you to tell me how to become more spiritual?"

These are all understandable responses. Each of us has perhaps resisted guidance from fellow Christians somewhere in our faith journey. We are not always receptive to the various ways God seeks to help us grow.

As class leaders we must be sure that we do not unknowingly carry an air of superiority. We can prepare ourselves through prayer, admitting our weakness to God and asking for guidance in projecting his image as we go to do his work.

It often takes time to trust, and being a class member requires trust in the leader and trust in God. This trust must be freely given and not forced by the leader. In Romans 12:16 we are reminded, "Live in harmony with one another; do not be haughty, but associate with the lowly; do not claim to be wiser than you are."

We may remind our reluctant member that the worship service alone does not prepare us with clear-cut guidelines for a disciplined Christian journey. While the pastor may not have the time to work with each person individually, other laypeople can help us stay on a course of spiritual growth.

When class members decide to be intentional about their spiritual growth, God helps them each step of the way. As a class leader you can encourage them not only to read the Bible and pray for others but also to balance their growth in the areas of compassion, worship, and justice for others. Many will appreciate the friendly nudge and will invite the Holy Spirit to invade their lives in new ways, thus allowing themselves to experience the guidance and love of God as never before.

So, class leaders, don't give up on your class members. Continue to call them regularly, offer to share additional material, invite them to attend a Covenant Discipleship Group meeting with you, and nurture them in love. You never know what is going on in someone else's life. A member may be ready or even excited about getting started. By the same token, do not get perturbed if a member asks you to stop calling. All things happen in God's time, and you can still continue to pray for the person.

## Reports From Class Leaders

**Bill and Thelma Johnson—**
**Asbury United Methodist Church, Washington, DC**

Bill explains how they function as a couple: "We have twenty-two families; we each take half. We accept people where they are. Some are ready to go [with their Spiritual direction]; others are not. When they seem ready to grasp the full covenant, we will encourage their participation in Covenant Discipleship Groups. However, there is no pressure to succeed. We visit people in their homes, on the phone, at church, and in other places. We have had great success with group meetings too. We fellowship and talk individually to the people gathered."

On spiritual direction, Thelma says, "We keep before our members the General Rule of Discipleship and ask them, 'Will you be willing to commit to one clause under each area of discipline?' We give them a list of clauses and suggest that they choose one from each of the four areas or construct their own. I explain that as Covenant Discipleship members, Bill and I are committed to several clauses and give an account each week. Class members give an account to us once a month when we ask, 'How are you doing?' We are simply a guide or support."

**Fred and Ann Price—**
**Asbury United Methodist Church, Washington, DC**

Class leaders ministry means the following to them: "It lets us help others as they seek balance in their daily lives. It is an avenue for us to become personally involved in the spiritual direction of a small segment of the congregation who may not always have contact with or know of church activities. It provides enhanced opportunity for personal witnessing. It enables us to take Covenant Discipleship mutual accountability to another level. It enables us to be more attuned to the personal and spiritual needs of members of the congregation and helps us extend the pastor's efforts to 'touch' and provide assistance to church members. It provides opportunities for personal growth as we develop skills that will help us be successful class leaders, such as listening, developing win-win situations, and seeking a spiritual sense of community. This program has provided another opportunity for us to work together as a couple."

**Sandra King-Shaw—**
**Asbury United Methodist Church, Washington, DC**

Sandra King-Shaw, on being the coordinator of Covenant Discipleship and class leaders at Asbury Church since its inception, says, "I have a passion for what I am doing. I have had things that have had an impact on my life for a short while, but I don't know how many experiences I have had that have moved me as profoundly as Covenant Discipleship and class leader. As a result of what I have experienced, I say to others, 'I promise you, you'll change.'

"As a Christian, I've always been involved in working in the church. There were many things I was already doing—praying, studying the Bible, ushering, and trying to help others; but Covenant Discipleship made me change why I do it, how I see my life, and how I see people. It has made me mission-focused. And each year it has a deeper effect on me. I feel the same about class leaders. I am more aware of what I was or was not doing for God.

"I asked Reverend Matthews if I could continue as the coordinator a little longer for three reasons. There is this passion in me to do it better. I want to be sure both ministries are well-grounded in Asbury so that the next person will not have to do repair but can move them to their next level. I don't hear any other call as I hear this call; maybe it's because I now feel accountable for my discipleship.

"As a class leader, I tell my members where I started and the steps I am taking every day. I ask them to make a conscious decision to take a next step in their spiritual journey. I want to walk with them, and I need them to walk with me as we share experiences and encourage each other. I feel closer to others than I have felt in my other experiences in the church. I know I must move on and leave this job to the next person, but for right now it will not let me go, and I don't want to let it go."

## Benefits of Class Leaders Ministry

Dr. Eugene Matthews of Asbury Church says, "The ministry of class leaders, coupled with the Covenant Discipleship Groups, has made a difference in the Asbury congregation. Although the number of class leaders and Covenant Discipleship Groups is not sufficient for our congregation, the entire congregation is aware of these two programs. The church members also realize that the major focus has been placed upon a spiritual base: centering upon the mandate to make disciples for Christ.

"The selection of people who serve as Asbury's class leaders has been vital in establishing a climate and mindset that have brought us to the threshold of the changes necessary for ministry and mission as we prepare to move into the twenty-first century."

# Part

# 3

*Additional Helps*

# The General Rules

In the latter end of the year 1739 eight or ten persons came to Mr. Wesley, in London, who appeared to be deeply convinced of sin, and earnestly groaning for redemption. They desired, as did two or three more the next day, that he would spend some time with them in prayer, and advise them how to flee from the wrath to come, which they saw continually hanging over their heads. That he might have more time for this great work, he appointed a day when they might all come together, which from thenceforward they did every week, namely, on Thursday in the evening. To these, and as many more as desired to join with them (for their number increased daily), he gave those advices from time to time which he judged most needful for them, and they always concluded their meeting with prayer suited to their several necessities.

This was the rise of the **United Society**, first in Europe, and then in America. Such a society is no other than "a company of men having the *form* and seeking the *power* of godliness, united in order to pray together, to receive the word of exhortation, and to watch over one another in love, that they may help each other to work out their salvation."

That it may the more easily be discerned whether they are indeed working out their own salvation, each society is divided into smaller companies, called **classes,** according to their respective places of abode. There are about twelve persons in a class, one of whom is styled the **leader.** It is his duty:

1. To see each person in his class once a week at least, in order: (1) to inquire how their souls prosper; (2) to advise, reprove, comfort or exhort, as occasion may require; (3) to receive what they are willing to give toward the relief of the preachers, church, and poor.

2. To meet the ministers and the stewards of the society once a week, in order: (1) to inform the minister of any that are sick, or of any that walk disorderly and will not be reproved; (2) to pay the stewards what they have received of their several classes in the week preceding.

There is only one condition previously required of those who desire admission into these societies: "a desire to flee from the wrath to come, and to be saved from their sins." But wherever this is really fixed in the soul it will be shown by its fruits.

It is therefore expected of all who continue therein that they should continue to evidence their desire of salvation,

*First:* By doing no harm, by avoiding evil of every kind, especially that which is most generally practiced, such as: . . . [*What follows is a list of generally practiced evil in Wesley's time.*]

(From *The Book of Discipline of The United Methodist Church—1996.* Copyright © 1996 by The United Methodist Publishing House. Used by permission. Pages 69–72.)

It is expected of all who continue in these societies that they should continue to evidence their desire of salvation,

*Secondly:* By doing good; by being in every kind merciful after their power; as they have opportunity, doing good of every possible sort, and, as far as possible, to all men: . . .
[*What follows is a list of ways of doing good.*]

It is expected of all who desire to continue in these societies that they should continue to evidence their desire of salvation,

*Thirdly:* By attending upon all the ordinances of God; such are:

The public worship of God.

The ministry of the Word, either read or expounded.

The Supper of the Lord.

Family and private prayer.

Searching the Scriptures.

Fasting or abstinence.

(From *The Book of Discipline of The United Methodist Church—1996*. Copyright © 1996 by The United Methodist Publishing House. Used by permission. Pages 69–72.)

# The Church's Primary Task

The church's mission in every age has been to make disciples of Jesus Christ and to send these disciples forth into the world. The world is where people live their daily lives—at home, at work, and in the varied social, cultural, and political settings within their local community, the nation, and the world.

Jesus' closing words in the Gospel of Matthew (28:19-20) serve as the foundation for this mission: "Go therefore and make disciples of all nations, baptizing them in the name of the Father and of the Son and of the Holy Spirit, and teaching them to obey everything that I have commanded you. And remember, I am with you always, to the end of the age." The mission to make disciples is our grace-filled response to Jesus' announcement of God's reign in the world. This mission is the church's primary task.

The process for carrying out this mission involves:

- reaching out into the world and proclaiming the gospel in ways that seek, welcome and gather people into Christ's body, the church;
- encouraging people in their relationship to Christ and inviting them to commit their lives to God through Jesus Christ;
- nurturing people as Christian disciples through worship, study, prayer, and other disciplines of the faith;
- sending people forth and supporting them as they live and act as faithful disciples in the world.

This mission is a dynamic, interactive, ongoing process. Each aspect flows into all the others. Each aspect is mutually dependent on all the others. No single aspect is more important than another. They are all equally a part of the congregation's total system for mission. They are not a loose collection of tasks in which congregations are engaged, but are aspects of the church's *one* primary task: to make disciples.

Congregations have sometimes focused on one of these functions to the neglect of the others. . . . Reaching out and inviting, nurturing and discipling, and sending forth and supporting all form one interdependent system. All are essential if congregations are to fulfill their mission to the communities they serve.

The congregation is involved at the same time in every aspect of the one primary task of making disciples. . . . Although congregational leaders may have responsibilities for and interest in particular parts of the church's primary missional task, it is essential to see how their own interests and responsibilities fit within the larger framework of this primary task. It is equally important that they work with other leaders to ensure that the total system for making disciples—and not their particular responsibility alone—is vital and effective.

(*Job Descriptions and Leadership Training for Local Church Leaders: 1997–2000*, by Thomas R. Hawkins; © 1997 by Discipleship Resources, Nashville, TN; booklet, page 24.)

# Sample Job Description for a Class Leader

## The Primary Task of a Class Leader

To give leadership to a pastoral subgrouping of the congregation (a class) by helping the group witness to Jesus Christ in the world and to follow his teachings through acts of compassion, justice, worship, and devotion—under the guidance of the Holy Spirit.

## Opportunities for Your Congregation

As you begin to think about the focus for your work, reflect on these questions. Your responses will help you consider how the people of your congregation might live as faithful Christians in the world. These questions are best used in dialogue and discussion with other leaders of your congregation and larger community.

1. In what ways can you and your class members witness to Jesus Christ in the world?
2. In what specific acts of justice and compassion can you and your class members engage in your community?
3. How can your worship and devotional life help you walk with Christ in the world?
4. What role can your discipleship play in the quality of life of your congregation and the larger community?
5. In addition to your weekly Covenant Discipleship Group, how can you prepare for the role of class leader?

My vision for the discipleship of my class members:

_____

_____

I will prepare myself for the leadership of my class by:

_____

_____

## Responsibilities of a Class Leader

*(NOTE: Your class is a pastoral subgrouping of the congregation. It is not like a Sunday school or continuing education class.)*

1. To keep focused on the primary task.
2. To be accountable for your own walk with Christ by meeting weekly in a Covenant Discipleship Group.

(From *Job Descriptions and Leadership Training for Local Church Leaders: 1997–2000*, by Thomas R. Hawkins; © 1997 by Discipleship Resources, Nashville, TN; leaflet 32.)

3. To encourage your class members to practice justice, compassion, worship, and devotion, as they witness to Christ in the world.
4. To "nudge" your class members in their discipleship by upholding them through regular telephone calls, letters, or personal visits.
5. To guide your class members in finding resources for their acts of worship, devotion, justice, compassion, and their witness to Jesus Christ.
6. To meet once a month with the pastor, the lay leader, and other class leaders in a regularly scheduled leaders' meeting.
7. To keep alert for the promptings of the Holy Spirit in your life.
8. To participate in the church council (council on ministries) if requested.
9. To be accountable to the congregation through your annual election to the office of class leader at charge conference.

## Getting Started

1. Take a second look at your responses in the Opportunities section. Or, if you have not answered these questions, take time to do so now.
2. If you do not already belong to a Covenant Discipleship Group in your congregation, you should join one as soon as possible.
3. Attend the regularly scheduled leaders' meeting each month. This will help you learn how to assist your class members with their discipleship.
4. Investigate and list suggestions for your class members to practice acts of compassion, justice, worship, and devotion as they witness to Christ in the world.
5. Learn the discipleship patterns of each member of your class so that you can help in appropriate ways. Each member will need different assistance.
6. Study *Guidelines for Leading Your Congregation: Leading as a Class Leader 1997–2000* (see "Covenant Discipleship Resources," page 60).
7. Participate in seminars offered to class leaders through your annual conference, United Methodist seminaries and schools of theology, and the General Board of Discipleship.

## Skills and Interests Helpful for Your Job

1. A willingness to be held accountable for your own discipleship.
2. An understanding of what it means to witness to Christ in the world and to practice compassion, devotion, justice, and worship.
3. An ability to listen to and communicate with people of all ages.
4. A plan to contact your class members on a regular basis so that you can "watch over them in love" (John Wesley).
5. A love of Jesus Christ, a commitment to the gospel, and a dedication to the life of active discipleship.

## Training for Your Job

A class leader does not require special training. Being involved each day in witnessing to Jesus Christ in the world and following Christ's teachings through acts of compassion, jus-

(From *Job Descriptions and Leadership Training for Local Church Leaders: 1997–2000*, by Thomas R. Hawkins; © 1997 by Discipleship Resources, Nashville, TN; leaflet 32.)

tice, worship, and devotion provides you with the best kind of training—training on the job. Being accountable in a weekly Covenant Discipleship Group teaches you the best kind of leadership—leadership by example.

## People and Agencies That Can Help

- Your pastor.
- Other class leaders in your congregation and in other congregations.
- The members of your Covenant Discipleship Group.
- Other lay and clergy women and men who are recognized for their witness to Christ and their works of devotion, compassion, justice, and worship.

(From *Job Descriptions and Leadership Training for Local Church Leaders: 1997–2000*, by Thomas R. Hawkins; © 1997 by Discipleship Resources, Nashville, TN; leaflet 32.)

To witness to Jesus Christ
in the world, and to follow
his teachings through acts
of compassion, justice,
worship, and devotion,
under the guidance of the Holy Spirit.

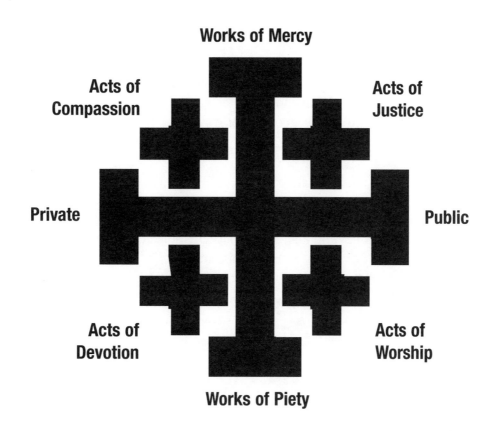

Works of Mercy

Acts of
Compassion

Acts of
Justice

Private

Public

Acts of
Devotion

Acts of
Worship

Works of Piety

# Sample Covenant Clauses

### Devotions

I will

- practice daily devotions, including the reading of Scripture and prayer;
- begin each day praising and thanking God for the gift of life and the potential of good therein;
- read articles and books that will enable me to grow in the knowledge and love of God;
- pray for people to whom I've been unjust or who have wronged me;
- keep a daily gratitude journal in which I record five things I am thankful for.

### Justice

I will

- speak out whenever I am aware of God's justice being ignored;
- express disapproval of racial, social, and sexual prejudice among relatives and friends;
- be sensitive to injustice and devote my prayers, time, and resources to alleviate them;
- make an effort to get to know people of other ethnic backgrounds in my church, community, or workplace.

### Compassion

I will

- do all I can to help people in need;
- express feelings of genuine appreciation to at least one person each day;
- spend time each week helping disadvantaged people and/or someone in need;
- visit the elderly in a nursing home once a month;
- work at a clothes closet or food pantry at the church.

### Worship

I will

- return to God the first tenth of all that I receive;
- be faithful and vigilant in my attendance and participation in worship each Sunday and give an account of those Sundays when I am absent;
- pray for those who visit our worship service, that they will be touched by grace;
- receive the sacrament of Holy Communion at least once a month.

# Sample Agenda
# for Class Leaders Council Meeting

| Agenda Item | Time | Notes |
|:---:|:---:|:---:|
| Fellowship | | |
| Welcome | | |
| Devotions | | |
| News of Joy and Sadness | | |
| Spiritual Direction | | |
| Status of Class Members | | |
| Prayers for All | | |
| General Information and Announcements | | |
| Words of Wisdom and Closing Prayer | | |

# Sample Introductory Letter

Dear (*name of person*):

This letter is written to inform you that (*name of church*) United Methodist Church has embarked upon an ambitious and strategic plan to connect with and care for all of our members. This plan will link every member of the congregation with a class leader. Each class leader is appointed by the senior pastor to serve as a "co-minister" and will have the responsibility to witness for Christian discipleship to a small group of fifteen to twenty people in the congregation by encouraging, guiding, and watching over them. Additionally, this individual will serve as a source of information for his or her class members regarding the ministry, life, and work of the congregation.

I have been assigned to serve as your class leader. I am very excited about the possibilities that our relationship may hold for the future ministry of our church. You can anticipate a call from me within the next few weeks. I will be happy to further explain the nature and purpose of my office and welcome you to my class. If you are at church on Sunday, (*date*), I will be glad to see you in person and talk briefly with you after the service. I further invite you to call me at any time. My phone number is (*phone number*). May God continue to strengthen and keep you.

Grace and Peace,
(*class leader's name*)

# Sample Monthly Contact Form

**Month** _____

**Class members following the General Rule of Discipleship**

| Name | Devotion | Worship | Compassion | Justice |
|------|----------|---------|------------|---------|
|      |          |         |            |         |

# Words of Inspiration
# for Class Leaders and Class Members

Jesus came and said to them [the disciples], "All authority in heaven and on earth has been given to me. Go therefore and make disciples of all nations, baptizing them in the name of the Father and of the Son and of the Holy Spirit, and teaching them to obey everything that I have commanded you. And remember, I am with you always, to the end of the age." (Matthew 28:18-20)

Jesus said to Simon Peter, "Simon son of John, do you love me more than these?" He said to him, "Yes, Lord; you know that I love you." Jesus said to him, "Feed my lambs."

(John 21:15)

When it was evening, the disciples came to him [Jesus] and said, "This is a deserted place, and the hour is now late; send the crowds away so that they may go into the villages and buy food for themselves." Jesus said to them, "They need not go away; you give them something to eat." They replied, "We have nothing here but five loaves and two fish." And he said, "Bring them here to me." . . . Taking the five loaves and the two fish, he looked up to heaven, and blessed and broke the loaves, and gave them to the disciples, and the disciples gave them to the crowds. And all ate and were filled; and they took up what was left over of the broken pieces, twelve baskets full. (Matthew 14:15-20)

And they asked him [Jesus], "Is it lawful to cure on the sabbath?" . . . He said to them, "Suppose one of you has only one sheep and it falls into a pit on the sabbath; will you not lay hold of it and lift it out? How much more valuable is a human being than a sheep!"

(Matthew 12:10-12)

"I am the good shepherd. The good shepherd lays down his life for the sheep. . . . I know my own and my own know me, just as the Father knows me and I know the Father. . . . I have other sheep that do not belong to this fold. I must bring them also, and they will listen to my voice. So there will be one flock, one shepherd." (John 10:11, 14b-16)

My help comes from the LORD,
who made heaven and earth.
(Psalm 121:2)

But Moses said to God, "Who am I that I should go to Pharaoh, and bring the Israelites out of Egypt?" He [God] said, "I will be with you." . . . "I will be with your mouth and teach you what you are to speak." (Exodus 3:11-12a, 4:12)

And whatever you do, in word or deed, do everything in the name of the Lord.
(Colossians 3:17)

# Prayers

The following prayers have been included to remind us that our journey in becoming disciples is not ours alone. Many who have gone before us and who walk with us today share their words and inspirations with us.


Dear God,

Thank you for this time with you away from the busyness of our lives so that we can focus our minds and hearts on what is truly important. Sometimes we forget to spend time talking and listening to you and doing what you have called us to do—make disciples of ourselves and others. Though we haven't been consistent in doing your will, you keep on giving us another day to do it better.

Bless all people and all groups committed to being your representatives in the world. Give us new hearing, new vision, and a new understanding of our need to lead and give service to others. Rejuvenate us and send us back into the world intentional about being your disciples. Bless the world, dear God; it is yours. Fix it where it needs fixing, and give us the strength and courage to brighten the corners where we are, so that we may help create that new world that is pressing in on us. Amen.

(Grace Bradford)


Here am I; send me!
(Isaiah 6:8)


Lord, let me not live to be useless!
(John Wesley, *Journal from October
29, 1762, to May 25, 1765*)

Lord, in my ministry as a class leader,
teach me to . . .
pray your way,
obey your way,
insist on your way,
take risks your way,
lead your way,
feed your way,
live your way,
forgive your way.
I give thanks to you for showing me
every day, YOUR WAY. Amen.

(Grace Bradford)

I am no longer my own, but thine.
Put me to what thou wilt, rank me with whom thou wilt.
Put me to doing, put me to suffering.
Let me be employed by thee or laid aside for thee,
exalted for thee or brought low by thee.
Let me be full, let me be empty.
Let me have all things, let me have nothing.
I freely and heartily yield all things
to thy pleasure and disposal.
And now, O glorious and blessed God,
Father, Son, and Holy Spirit,
thou art mine, and I am thine. So be it.
And the covenant which I have made on earth,
let it be ratified in heaven. **Amen.**

("A Covenant Prayer in the Wesleyan Tradition," from
*The United Methodist Hymnal*, copyright © 1989
The United Methodist Publishing House; 607.)

# An Order for the Commissioning of Class Leaders

*This order is intended for the public commissioning of class leaders following their appointment by a Charge or Church Conference of the congregation.*

*The order may be led by the pastor of the congregation, the district superintendent, or the bishop of the area.*

*As a Response to the Word or at some other appropriate place within a service of congregational worship, the pastor invites the newly appointed class leader(s) to come forward.*

*Pastor to congregation:*

Dear friends,
the office of class leader is one of the most important contributions
   made by world Methodism
      to the pastoral leadership of Christ's holy Church.

In the General Rules of 1743,
   John Wesley described the Methodist societies
   as companies of men and women who,
"having the form, and seeking the power of godliness,"
came together in order to pray,
   to receive the word of exhortation,
   and "to watch over one another in love
      that they may help each other work out their salvation."
To this end, the societies were divided into small companies, called classes,
   each with an appointed leader
   "to advise, reprove, comfort, or exhort, as occasion may require."

Class leaders of today continue this tradition.
In the founding *Discipline* of our church, they are described as persons
   "not only of sound judgment, but truly devoted to God,"
     who are willing to help others in the congregation
     "to grow in the knowledge and love of God."

*Pastor to class leader(s):*

Do you accept the office of class leader
   in this congregation of The United Methodist Church?

**I do.**

(From *The United Methodist Book of Worship,* © 1992 The United Methodist Publishing House. Used by permission. Pages 602–604.)

Will you exercise this office
by helping other members of the congregation
    to fulfill the general rule of discipleship:
To witness to Jesus Christ in the world, and to follow his teachings
    through acts of compassion, justice, worship, and devotion,
    under the guidance of the Holy Spirit?

**I will.**

Will you help other members of the congregation
    to be accountable for their discipleship,
    not by judging them, but by watching over them in love?

**I will.**

Will you meet weekly in covenant with others of like mind
    and purpose to be accountable for your own discipleship?

**I will.**

*Pastor to congregation:*

Will you affirm the call of *these men and women* to be *class leaders*
    in this congregation of The United Methodist Church?

**We will.**

Will you acknowledge *them* as your *leaders* in discipleship,
    and accept *their* guidance as *they* watch over you in love?

**We will.**

*Pastor to class leader(s):*

You are hereby commissioned as *class leaders*
    in this congregation of The United Methodist Church.

Let us pray.

Most gracious God,
    bless your servant(s)
    whom we now entrust with the office of class leader.
Grant *them* wisdom tempered by your love,
    and courage tempered by your justice,
    so that Jesus Christ might be honored and served
        by all in this congregation,
    to the furtherance of your coming reign, on earth as in heaven;
through the same Jesus Christ our Lord. **Amen.**

UMH *438, "Forth in Thy Name, O Lord," may then be sung.*

(From *The United Methodist Book of Worship*, © 1992 The United
Methodist Publishing House. Used by permission. Pages 602–604.)

# Covenant Discipleship Resources

*Accountable Discipleship: Living In God's Household*, by Steve Manskar (Discipleship Resources, available in 2000).

*CD Journal: A Guide for Covenant Discipleship Groups on Campus*. Available through the Campus Ministry Section, General Board of Higher Education and Ministry, P.O. Box 871, Nashville, TN 37202.

*Class Leaders: Recovering a Tradition*, by David Lowes Watson (Discipleship Resources, 1991).

*Class Meetings Workbook for United Methodists: For use in the New York West Area of The United Methodist Church*, by Bishop Hae-Jong Kim (self-printed).

*Covenant Discipleship: Christian Formation Through Mutual Accountability*, by David Lowes Watson (Discipleship Resources, 1991).

*Covenant Discipleship Quarterly* is a quarterly newsletter for members of Covenant Discipleship Groups. You can receive a free subscription by writing to Covenant Discipleship Quarterly, P.O. Box 840, Nashville, TN 37202-0840; by calling 615-340-7144; by faxing 615-340-7071, Attention: JoAnn Eslinger—Covenant Discipleship Quarterly; or by e-mailing **jeslinger@gbod.org**.

*Forming Christian Disciples: The Role of Covenant Discipleship and Class Leaders in the Congregation*, by David Lowes Watson (Discipleship Resources, 1991).

*Guidelines for Leading Your Congregation: Leading as Class Leader 1997–2000*, by Phyllis Tyler (Abingdon Press, 1996).

*Journal for Covenant Discipleship: A Weekly Record for Covenant Discipleship Groups*, edited by Marigene Chamberlain (1991). Available through the Office of Accountable Discipleship, General Board of Discipleship, P.O. Box 840, Nashville, TN 37202.

*Sprouts: Nurturing Children Through Covenant Discipleship*, by Edie Genung Harris and Shirley L. Ramsey (Discipleship Resources, 1995).

*Together In Love: Covenant Discipleship With Youth*, by David Sutherland (Discipleship Resources, 1999).

# Other Helpful Resources

*A Longing for Holiness: Selected Writings of John Wesley* (Upper Room Spiritual Classics, Series 1), edited by Keith Beasley-Topliffe (Upper Room Books, 1997).

*Come to the Waters: Baptism and Our Ministry of Welcoming Seekers and Making Disciples*, by Daniel T. Benedict, Jr. (Discipleship Resources, 1996).

*Job Descriptions and Leadership Training for Local Church Leaders: 1997–2000*, by Thomas R. Hawkins (Discipleship Resources, 1997).

*Claiming All Things for God: Prayer, Discernment, and Ritual for Social Change*, by George D. McLain (Abingdon Press, 1998).

*The Life You've Always Wanted: Spiritual Disciplines for Ordinary People*, by John Ortberg (Zondervan Publishing House, 1997).

*The Message*, by Eugene H. Peterson (NavPress, 1993).

*The Book of Discipline of The United Methodist Church—1996* (The United Methodist Publishing House, 1996).

*The United Methodist Book of Worship* (The United Methodist Publishing House, 1992).

*Illuminata: Thoughts, Prayers, Rites of Passage*, by Marianne Williamson (Random House, Inc., 1994).

# Agencies and Organizations

### General Board of Discipleship

P.O. Box 840

Nashville, TN 37202-0840

Phone 615-340-7200

Fax 615-340-7006

### Discipleship Resources

P.O. Box 840

Nashville, TN 37202-0840

For information, call 800-814-7833.

To order, call 800-685-4370 or fax 770-442-9742.

### Cokesbury

201 Eighth Avenue, South

P.O. Box 801

Nashville, TN 37202

For information, contact Curric-U-Phone at 800-251-8591.

To order, call 800-672-1789 or fax 800-445-8189.

# Accountable Discipleship Canopy

Class leaders are part of a larger ministry of accountable discipleship. The diagram below indicates the many forms and settings that fall within the canopy of accountable discipleship. If you are interested in finding out more about any of the groups listed below, contact the Office of Accountable Discipleship, General Board of Discipleship, P.O. Box 840, Nashville, TN 37202-0840.

# Notes